Baby Sign Language
Teaching Guide

Table of Contents

Foreword

"Baby, what are you thinking?" Have you ever looked into those beautiful eyes and wondered what was going on in that little head? If the urge to communicate didn't strike during one of those peaceful moments, perhaps Baby's crying made you ask, "Baby, why are you fussing?"

I remember being desperately impatient to know my daughter's thoughts and how she perceived the world around her. I felt particularly desperate when she would cry out in distress and I was unable to understand the cause, and therefore helpless to end her despair. I was drawn to Baby Sign Language because I wanted to communicate with her. I wanted to share her joys during the happy moments and ease her distress during the difficult moments. If Baby Sign Language could help me communicate earlier and more effectively with my daughter, then it was worth a try. It turned out even better than I had hoped.

Babies are brilliant! Babies are much smarter than many people realize. Babies develop a basic understanding of language and their environment surprisingly early. Months before they can speak, babies are intricately aware of their surroundings. They just haven't developed the complex vocal control necessary to form spoken words and verbally express this awareness. But babies have good hand control, even at this early age, and can make simple gestures. This dexterity allows them to start communicating via sign language as young as six months old.

Baby Sign Language is incredibly useful. It allows your child to communicate in a constructive way with less fussing and whining. Knowing just five signs will make an immense difference. Your baby will be able to request milk or food, ask for a favorite toy, say he is ready for his bath, or tell you he is ready for bed. Even a small signing vocabulary dramatically reduces tantrums, decreases parental anxiety, and enables you to meet the child's immediate needs.

For example, my daughter was uncharacteristically fussy one afternoon. After a few minutes of fussing, she began to sign *cat*. We do not have a cat, but her grandmother had recently sent her a toy plush cat. We located the stuffed animal (she had left it under a chair) and she immediately stopped fussing. She just wanted her toy cat! I would never have guessed this was what was troubling her without Baby Sign Language. Who knows how long she would have continued to fuss if she had been unable to communicate her need.

Baby Sign Language also serves as a bonding activity, helping parents and their babies develop a closer connection. My favorite part of signing with my daughter is the insight it gives me into her point of view and how she experiences the world. I remember the first time she saw a horse and made the sign for *dog*. Suddenly, I saw the connection: in the world of a baby, those unfamiliar four-legged animals reminded her of our family dog. She was making sense of her surroundings in a thoughtful and creative way, and I could watch this process unfold.

In addition to the communication and bonding advantages, there are developmental benefits. Studies show that babies who learn sign language typically speak earlier, have larger vocabularies, and attain better educational outcomes.

It is a privilege to accompany your family on this wonderful journey through early childhood. I hope you find Baby Sign Language a useful tool and an enriching experience.

Lila Retnasaba

Founder, BabySignLanguage.com

Overview

This book is divided into nine chapters. Chapters progress from basic how-to information, to advanced techniques and specialized information. Start at the beginning of the book with our Quick Start Guide, then read those chapters most applicable to your needs and situation.

If you have questions or comments, email us at book@babysign-language.com or visit us at www.BabySignLanguage.com.

The chapters are as follows:

Chapter 1: Quick Start Guide

The Quick Start Guide is a condensed, action-oriented introduction to Baby Sign Language. This chapter provides the tools to start teaching Baby Sign Language immediately.

Chapter 2: The F.R.E.E. Method

The F.R.E.E. Method is our common sense approach to learning and teaching Baby Sign Language. We explore the core concepts of Fun, Repetition, Encouragement, and Expansion.

Chapter 3: Five Stages of Signing Development

Learn the five stages your baby will go through as she learns to sign. This will help you monitor the baby's progress and know when to move to the next stage.

Chapter 4: Getting Everyone Involved

Get friends, family, and caregivers involved in signing. This gives your baby more teachers and more opportunities to practice.

Chapter 5: Advanced Teaching Methods

Incorporate teaching aids such as flash cards and figurines into your sign language lessons. Learn how to achieve faster results by modeling signs using the Pepperberg Method.

Chapter 6: Signing Phrases

Teach your baby to combine two or more signs to create phrases. Enable Baby to unleash his creativity and establish the foundation for communicating using sentences.

Chapter 7: Signing During the Toddler Years

Use Baby Sign Language to prevent the "terrible twos" by reducing frustration and giving your baby more control over her environment.

Chapter 8: Speaking and Signing

Transition to verbal communication. Use Baby Sign Language to help your baby speak sooner and with more confidence.

Chapter 9: Signing Beyond Babyhood

Continue developing sign language beyond the baby years.
Progress toward fluency in sign language.

Chapter One
Quick Start Guide

By the end of this chapter you will be ready to teach sign language to your baby. The Quick Start Guide introduces the basics of Baby Sign Language along with our approach to teaching. We cover:

- **Basic Principles** - our parent-centric approach to teaching Baby Sign Language

- **First Signs** - choosing five starter signs that are suitable for your child

- **Learning New Signs** - how to learn new signs and use them with your baby

- **Coaching** - techniques for helping your baby learn to sign

Basic Principles

The Parent-Focused Approach

We take a parent-focused approach because you, the parent, are your baby's first and most influential teacher. Babies constantly observe and imitate their parents and caregivers. Consequently, the best way for your baby to learn sign language is for you to teach her.

For most parents, Baby Sign Language is their first experience on the teaching end of formal education. This will be fun! Babies love figuring stuff out. Watch the excitement ripple through your baby's body when things start to click. Hear the shrieks of delight when signs first come together. You will be inspired!

This book prepares you for your new role as head coach. We will walk you through the basics of Baby Sign Language and equip you to be an effective coach for your baby. We hope these teaching skills will be useful well beyond Baby Sign Language.

Parents play the role of head coach for their young children.

The F.R.E.E. Method

The F.R.E.E. acronym is an easy way to remember the core tenets of Baby Sign Language. F.R.E.E. stands for:

- Fun

- Repeat

- Encourage

- Expand

Fun is Number One

Make the experience FUN for Baby and FUN for you. You will have greater success when learning is an enjoyable experience. How can you make signing fun? Be playful with your signing and incorporate signing into books, songs, and games.

Repeat Repeat Repeat

REPETITION is critical to signing success. Babies learn most of their behavior from imitation, so make signing a natural part of your daily communication. Incorporating sign language into your routines gives Baby lots of exposure without you needing to set aside separate time. The more exposure you give your baby to signs, the easier it will be for her to start making the connection between signs and meaning.

Encourage Baby's Progress

ENCOURAGE any success with plenty of attention. Claps, hugs, kisses, encouraging words, and exclamations of glee are motivators for learning. Baby loves your attention and understanding, so when she starts signing back, be sure to offer plenty of encouragement. Even if the first signs aren't perfect, praise any progress and soon you will have a signing enthusiast.

Expand Your Signing Vocabulary

Continuously EXPAND your signing vocabulary. Once Baby has started to grasp her first few signs, add new signs. Focus on the signs that are most useful and interesting to your baby.

First Signs

Choosing Your First Signs

Focus on a few signs at first. We suggest starting with five signs. Focusing initial efforts on just five signs makes learning the signs easier for both you and your baby. Attempting to learn too many signs at the outset can be overwhelming. Give yourself time to learn a few signs and develop the habit of using them. Later, you can add more signs to your repertoire.

In the next section we will cover ten popular "starter" signs. We explain how to pick starter signs that will resonate with your child.

*Starter signs should represent words that are
frequently used, clear, and memorable.*

Any signs can be used to start, but the best results are achieved when starting with signs that are frequently used, clear, and memorable.

Frequently Used

Choose signs that will have many opportunities for use in your daily routine. *Food* and *milk* are good examples of frequently used signs because they can be used every time your child eats or drinks. The sign for *dentist* is an example of a poor starter sign because you are not likely to use *dentist* frequently throughout the day. Infrequently used words can be added eventually, but in the beginning stick to signs that can be used multiple times per day.

Remember, you are developing a signing habit for yourself as well as your baby. Selecting signs you can use many times per day helps you remember to sign and helps you form the habit of signing. Once signing becomes habitual for you, your baby will start signing back when developmentally able. Once Baby is signing back, gradually add more signs to your signing vocabulary.

Clear

The first signs should also have simple and clear meanings that are easy for Baby to grasp. Nouns are particularly easy, especially those representing important people (e.g., *mom* or *dad*) or significant everyday objects (e.g., *food* or *milk*). Avoid signs representing feelings like *happy* or *sad*. Emotional signs are difficult to teach in the beginning because their meanings are vague and complex. Also, avoid *please* and *thank you* when selecting first signs. While learning courteous behavior is a part of healthy development, the concept does not mean anything to a very young child.

Memorable

Starter signs should also be memorable and motivating for Baby. Choose words that represent significant things to Baby. Signs representing family members and food work well because they are important in a baby's life. Signs representing pets or other objects of fascination (e.g., *ceiling fans* or *balls*) are also good choices.

Beginner Signs - Choose Five

In this section we introduce ten starter signs and show you how to remember them. We also explain some great ways to teach each sign to your baby.

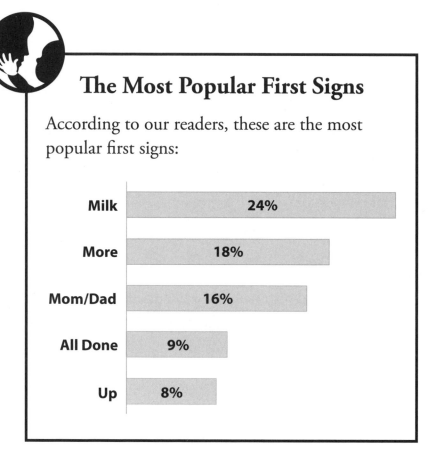

The Most Popular First Signs

According to our readers, these are the most popular first signs:

Sign	Percentage
Milk	24%
More	18%
Mom/Dad	16%
All Done	9%
Up	8%

To begin, choose five of the following signs that you want to learn. Remember, by concentrating your efforts on five signs and giving yourself plenty of opportunities for practice, you will quickly create a signing habit. There will be ample time to add more signs after you and your baby master the first five.

- Mom
- Dad
- More
- All Done
- Milk
- Water
- Eat
- Book
- Dog
- Cat

The next few pages explain each of these signs. Read the sections corresponding to the five signs you choose and skip the rest until you need them.

1. Mom

Mom is one of the most common first signs because of mom's importance and the fact that mom is often the primary caregiver.

Signing: To sign *mom*, extend and spread your fingers apart. With your pinkie facing forward, tap your thumb on your chin. The sign looks like a wave from the side.

The sign for *mom* is similar to the sign for *dad*, but lower on the face. Female signs are often similar to male signs, but the male variant is usually above the nose, and the female below the nose.

Early attempts at the sign may look like flailing hands. This is common as Baby is still working on moving each hand independently and does not have good control of her fingers.

Teaching: If you are the mom, make the sign every time you approach Baby. If your baby is fussing and calling for you, make the *mom* sign and give her a cheery smile, saying "it's mom."

Mom

2. Dad

Like *mom*, *dad* is a great starter sign because Baby's world revolves around her parents.

Signing: To sign *dad*, extend and spread your fingers apart. With your pinkie facing forward, tap your thumb on the middle of your forehead. The sign looks like a wave from the side.

The sign for *dad* is the same as the sign for *mom*, just on the forehead instead of the chin. Males signs are often similar to female signs - just positioned higher. (Don't blame us - we didn't create this convention.)

Teaching: If you are the dad, sign *dad* and say "dad" when you are approaching Baby. Your approach and the sound of the word are sure to get their attention. If you are not the dad, but see him approaching, point toward him, make the sign, and say the word. Ensure that Baby sees dad and sees you making the *dad* sign.

Dad

3. More

More is a popular first sign because it represents a simple and useful concept to Baby. Initially, *more* is used primarily in the context of food or drink to let Baby communicate when she wants additional food or drink. After Baby has learned the sign, usage can be expanded to numerous other contexts.

Signing: To sign *more*, put your fingers together with your thumb touching the tips of your fingers. Then bring your hands together and separate them repeatedly.

The sign looks like you are holding bits of food in your hands and tapping them together.

Teaching: Give Baby a piece of a cracker, then ask if she wants *more* before doling out another portion. Even if Baby does not sign back, repeat the *more* sign before giving her more. This establishes the association between the sign and getting another serving.

More

4. All Done

All done gives your baby the ability to communicate that she is finished with an activity without resorting to fussing. The sign is typically used during mealtime to indicate when Baby has eaten enough.

All done is the American Sign Language sign for *finished*.

Signing: Start with palms facing your shoulders, then turn your hands so that your palms are facing out. Think of a person at the table, totally full and flicking the extra portions away.

Teaching: When Baby is finished with her food or drink, swiftly remove the food, say "all done" and make the sign. Baby will soon realize that food or drink is removed when she signs *all done*.

All done and *more* are complementary signs and often taught together. Both signs allow Baby to exercise control during meals and avert tantrums at the table.

All Done

5. *Milk*

The *milk* sign is used for both breast feeding and bottle feeding. When using both feeding methods, you may use a separate sign like *bottle* for the bottle feeding. Initially, however, keep it simple and use the same sign for both.

Signing: Take your dominant hand and make it into a fist in front of your body. Open the fist, then clench the fist again. Repeat several times.

The *milk* sign resembles the motion of milking a cow (i.e., squeezing the udder, then releasing).

Teaching: Say "milk" and make the *milk* sign just before offering the bottle or breast. As Baby feeds, make the sign and say the word a few more times. Repeat the sign and word when Baby is finished. This offers multiple opportunities for Baby to associate the sign with milk.

Milk

6. Water

Water is only a useful starter sign for babies that are drinking both water and milk. Therefore, this sign is usually introduced to older babies.

Signing: To sign *water*, curl your pinkie and place the tip of your thumb on your pinkie nail. Extend your remaining fingers to create a "W" shape. Then bring the side of your hand (index finger side) toward your mouth and bounce the "W" off of your mouth.

The sign looks like you are making the letter "W" (for water) with your fingers and tapping the "W" on your mouth.

Teaching: Sign *water* when you give Baby a drink of water. Make the sign again as she drinks the water, then again when she finishes drinking.

You can also make the sign before and during bath time. Run water over Baby's hand while saying and signing *water*.

Water

7. Eat (food)

Eat is a universally popular sign and activity. *Eat* is a great starter sign because it represents a discrete action that Baby performs multiple times a day. *Eat* is often taught with *more* and *all done*. *Eat* can be the initiating sign for a meal while *more* and *all done* dictate the duration of the meal. *Eat* is also easy to model.

Signing: To sign *eat*, touch your thumb to your fingertips and bring your hand to your mouth. Slowly repeat bringing your thumb and fingers to your mouth.

The sign looks as though you are holding a morsel of food in your fingertips and bringing the food to your mouth.

Teaching: Sit Baby in her high chair, and before putting any food on the tray, sign *eat* a few times. Repeat the sign after Baby takes a bite of food. *Eat* can also be modeled as Baby watches you eat. Before taking a bite, sign *eat*, then take another bite of your food.

Eat

8. Book

Book is a favorite starter sign for multiple reasons. First, the sign closely resembles the action of reading a book. Second, books are easily accessible and children enjoy when parents read to them. Of course books are also a great platform to learn a lot of other signs.

Signing: To sign *book*, flatten your hands and put them together with palms and fingers touching. Open your hands with the pinkie side of your hands still touching as if they are hinged.

This sign looks like you are making a book with your hands and opening the book to read.

Teaching: Place a favorite book nearby. Sign *book* while speaking the word. Pick up and open the book so your baby can observe the resemblance between the sign and the object. Read the book to Baby, then close the book and repeat the sign.

Book

9. Dog

Children are fascinated with dogs and therefore excited to learn the sign. If you have a dog in your home then *dog* is an essential starter sign.

Even if you don't own a *dog*, you are likely to encounter dogs on walks or at a friend's house.

Signing: To sign *dog*, pat the side of your upper leg near your hip. The sign resembles the motion of an owner calling his dog.

Teaching: If you have a *dog* in your house, say the word dog then perform the sign whenever the dog enters the room and captures Baby's attention. This allows your baby to associate the sign with the animal.

If you don't have a dog at home, utilize flash cards, videos, or pictures to introduce the sign. Repeat the sign whenever you encounter a friendly dog to cement the learning.

Dog

10. Cat

Cat is a great beginner sign if you have a cat in the home. Children are drawn to cats because cats are much closer to a child's size, slink around, and have such interesting coats of fur.

Signing: To sign *cat*, touch your thumb and index finger together at the corner of your mouth and pull your hand away from your face.

The sign looks as though you are grabbing a long whisker and sliding your fingers down the full length of the whisker.

Teaching: With a cat at home, hold your baby in one arm and walk near your cat. Sign *cat* to your baby then point to the cat in the room.

You can point out the cat's whiskers to help your child associate the sign with the cat's whiskers. Animating the sign with a few meows can also help gain Baby's interest.

Cat

Learning New Signs

Look Up the Sign and Practice Along

A signing dictionary is a valuable resource as you learn Baby Sign Language. Video signing dictionaries are the first place to go when learning new signs. Pictures and drawings are useful reminders, but videos are the most helpful when learning a new sign. The BabySignLanguage.com website contains 600 of the most common signs (www.BabySignLanguage.com/dictionary). You can consult online ASL dictionaries (www.ASLpro.com or www.lifeprint.com) for less common signs.

Watch the video of the new sign several times focusing on the hand and finger placements and the motion. Practice as you watch to develop signing muscle memory.

Invent a Memory Trigger

Invent a little story or association that helps you remember each sign. Visualize the story in your head, making it as vivid, outrageous, and exaggerated as possible. The more outrageous the story, the more memorable it will be. For example, the sign for *girl* looks like the outline of a girl's bonnet strap. You can visualize a little girl tying the strap of a ridiculously oversized sun bonnet.

Stories make remembering the signs much easier and will etch the signs into your long-term memory. We provide memory triggers for the signs in our online dictionary, but inventing

The sign for "girl" looks like the outline of a bonnet strap.

your own is even better. It may seem awkward at first, but with practice, the signs will become ingrained in your memory and you will no longer need the story.

Use Your Dominant Hand

Use your dominant hand when making one-handed signs. For two-handed signs, the dominant hand typically makes the active motion and the non-dominant hand is passive.

Right-handed   *Left-handed*

Your dominant hand takes the active role in signing.

However, don't let proper hand usage stop you from signing. When using Baby Sign Language, you will often need to use the "wrong" hand. If you are right-handed and carrying your daughter with your right arm, use your left hand. While not technically correct, swapping hands is perfectly acceptable. Doing the sign is more valuable than using the correct hand. Remember, the goal is not perfect American Sign Language form, but communication.

Use Appropriate Tone of Voice

Signs are more interesting and informative if you use an animated tone of voice that is appropriate to the meaning of the sign. Exaggerate and enunciate the gesture, the spoken word, and the facial expression. For animal signs, imitate the animal. For emotion signs, act out the emotion. It would be confusing to sign *sad* with a peppy voice. And it would be a shame to sign *monkey* without acting like a monkey!

Practice Often

Practice makes perfect. However, you do not need to perfect the sign before teaching it to your baby. The more you repeat the sign, the quicker you will master its usage and the quicker Baby will start signing back.

Coaching Tips

When to Sign

The short answer: All The Time! You can never sign too much or too often!

The goal of our parent-focused approach is to make signing a natural and habitual component of your communication with your baby. Baby will copy you and learn through imitation.

The five signs you start with will correspond to objects and people that you and Baby are constantly in contact with, so use them often. Let's use the sign *milk* as an example. A baby nurses or takes a bottle many times throughout the day. Train yourself to sign *milk* every time you feed Baby. She is learning from this exposure, and just as importantly, you are developing your signing habit.

We start with only a handful of signs so that encounters with the chosen objects or people trigger a reminder to make the sign. For example, when you are breastfeeding, remember "oh yeah, I am supposed to make the *milk* sign."

You can never repeat a sign too often. Using the *milk* example, when feeding your baby, sign *milk* over and over again. You likely have her full attention during feeding sessions, so take advantage of the opportunity.

How to Teach Signs to Your Baby

Sign whenever you can. Babies are like sponges and soak in everything they see and hear, even when you think they're not paying attention. All signing is good signing, but there are a few tips for getting the best results when teaching your child.

Sign With Baby's Full Attention

Signs are most effective when you have Baby's full attention. A distracted baby will not fully absorb your teaching efforts. Find a quiet place to practice signing. If the television is on or a sibling is running around in the background, Baby's attention will not be on learning sign language.

A baby's attention span is short and prone to distraction. On some days, Baby will stay riveted. On other days, Baby will have no interest and her eyes will wander. Don't push too hard when Baby has the wiggles or is fussy. Conversely, keep signing on the days that she is interested.

A baby can still absorb signs even if only paying half attention, but it is most effective to teach a fully-attentive baby. So remove distractions whenever possible.

Placement

Try to place the sign in Baby's field of vision. She will usually look at your face, so take advantage of this by placing the sign just below your head. This placement ensures the sign is in her field of vision and automatically focuses Baby's attention on the sign. It also models for Baby where you want her to sign.

Place the sign in Baby's field of vision.

Using Their Hands

Help your baby form signs by gently manipulating her hands. Guiding her hands helps Baby develop the muscle memory for the sign.

Some babies let you shape their hands to make the signs, but many will not. If Baby resists, don't fight her. A baby that is resisting is not learning anything – her focus is on resisting you, not on learning the signs. Often you can simply try at another time when Baby is more relaxed. Alternatively, you can try the following technique.

Using Your Hands On Their Body

Use your hands to make the sign on or near Baby's body. For example, when making the *dog* sign, pat Baby's thigh. When signing *dad*, tap your thumb on Baby's head. This creates a tactile sensation associated with the word and teaches proper placement of the sign. This technique is particularly useful for babies with kinesthetic learning styles.

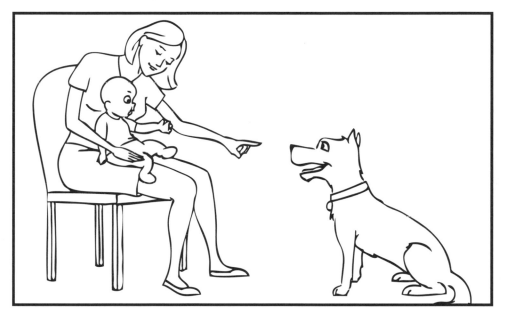

Making the sign for "dog" on the baby's body.

Timing and Speed

When teaching new signs, make signs slowly and exaggerate the motions. Also, remember to pause a few beats after each sign.

When American Sign Language (ASL) proficient adults sign, the movements are rapid and seem to blur into one another. However, when an ASL speaker is signing to a young child, the adult will slow their motions and exaggerate the signs, much like parents slow their speech when teaching a child to talk. The slow tempo and exaggerated motions make it easier for the child to understand and copy what is being communicated.

The pause at the end of each sign gives Baby a moment to register the sign. It also signals to Baby that your gesture was important. Finally, the pause separates the sign from motions that follow.

Speak and Sign Together

Sign and speak words at the same time. Just as you make slow exaggerated signs, you should slow down your speech and clearly articulate each syllable of the word to help Baby learn. It is crucial to pair the spoken and signed word. While Baby will rely on the signs at first, the end goal is to teach Baby to speak. Consequently, we want to sow the seeds for speaking so that when Baby is developmentally ready, the words will flow.

Chapter Two
The F.R.E.E. Method

The four basic principles of teaching Baby Sign Language are:

1. **Fun** - make it enjoyable so that Baby is motivated to learn how to sign

2. **Repetition** - repeat signs often to provide Baby many opportunities to observe and practice

3. **Encouragement** - provide calm encouragement to let Baby know when he is on the right track

4. **Expansion** - grow Baby's vocabulary to keep Baby challenged

The four basic principles of teaching Baby Sign Language are to make it Fun, incorporate Repetition, provide calm Encouragement, and continuously Expand the vocabulary. To remember these four principles we use the acronym F.R.E.E. (Fun, Repetition, Encouragement, Expansion). In this chapter we explore each of these four principles in detail.

Fun

Baby Sign Language is best undertaken as an entertaining addition to activities that parents enjoy with their children. You can sign while singing, playing games, reading your favorite book, taking a walk, eating dinner, and during almost every other activity with your baby. When your baby associates signing with fun, the experience will be enjoyable to you both and signing will become part of your daily routine. Once this positive association occurs, your baby will be much more motivated to sign.

Set the Tone

Babies take cues from their parents. Ever observed a baby fall down then look to his parent to decide whether or not to cry? If the parent remains calm, the baby is much more likely to remain calm. If the parent looks panicked, crying is sure to follow. The same concept applies when babies learn sign language. If the parent is having fun, the baby is sure to follow suit.

Many parents place unnecessary pressure on themselves to get their child signing as soon as possible. This is neither enjoyable nor productive. Remember that you are teaching a very young child. Don't worry if progress takes a little longer than you expect or if your child is not replicating signs perfectly. Babies often learn new signs and promptly forget them. Babies may sign a lot one day, then not sign at all the next. These "setbacks" are a normal part of their learning process. Enjoy the journey rather than emphasizing the destination. This leads to a more pleasant experience and a more effective learning environment.

The following tips can keep signing fun:

Incorporate Signs into Activities

The best signing lessons are those incorporated into daily activities with your baby. If you see a dog, sign *dog*. When you are eating, sign *eat*. Instead of dedicating only specific times to signing practice, sign throughout the day. Just like speaking, signing should become a natural part of communication with your baby.

Partner with a Signing Buddy

A signing buddy shares in the teaching experience and is a terrific resource when starting out. A signing buddy will increase your excitement for signing and create more opportunities for your baby to observe signs. You can also partner with your signing buddy to model signs for your baby.

Asking someone to be a signing buddy is a great way to engage a spouse, family member, or friend in what is sure to be a transformational experience for your baby. If your spouse is interested in Baby Sign Language, they are an ideal signing buddy. Other candidates include grandparents, a nanny or babysitter, older children, or close friends.

Celebrate Success

When you learn a new sign, celebrate. When Baby learns a new sign, celebrate. When Baby does something clever or cute while signing, celebrate. Get excited and tell everyone. Post it on your Facebook page, post it on our Facebook page (www.facebook.com/babysignlang/), tweet it, or share the video online for the whole family to enjoy. You may want to wait until signs are perfect or consistent, but don't. Friends and family members want to celebrate all of these small achievements with you.

Animate Your Signs

Infuse energy into your signs by projecting emotion and drama into the word accompanying each sign. Emphasize the spoken word and the gesture to bring the sign to life.

When signing an emotion, reflect that emotion with your voice and body language. When signing *sad*, make a long face, give a little pout, and drag out the word. Babies are good at reading your body language, so animating the sign in this way helps Baby understand the meaning of the word.

By wearing a sad look, the figure on the right
accurately represents the meaning of the word "sad".

Incorporating emotion is particularly useful when signing along to a story. For example, if you are reading a book and come across the word *lion*, growl and show off your best lion impression while making the sign. Your baby will not soon forget that part of the book or the sign. Baby will now look forward to the parts of the book where signs are used and will naturally want to participate by doing some signing of his own.

The sign for "monkey" is much more fun when you monkey about.

In summary, babies love liveliness, emotion, and drama, so use these elements to make signs more entertaining.

High Energy, Not Hyper

One small warning: keep the energy level high, but not hyper. In our excitement, parents often take things a little too far and start zooming Baby around the house like the Red Baron. Wild excitement is certainly fun and has a place in Baby's life. However, overstimulation does not facilitate learning and should be avoided.

continued

Often parents are guilty of creating a little too much excitement (which is why babies think parents are so much fun!). So, remember to maintain an atmosphere of calm energy when teaching Baby Sign Language.

So how do you infuse an appropriate energy level while avoiding overstimulation? Keep the level high enough that your baby focuses on the signs, but not so high that he loses focus and starts to break into hysterics.

Time and Place

Like adults, babies can be moody. Of course, this is not a revelation to any parent. Reading your child's mood will help you select the optimal time for signing sessions. Plan your practice sessions when Baby will be receptive. The worst time to engage your child in any developmental learning is when he is tired, hungry, or otherwise cranky. This applies to the parent as well as the child. When planning a more formal teaching session with flash cards or a book, the best times tend to be after Baby finishes a nap or following snack time.

Signing while your baby is engaged in a pleasant activity (eating, bathing, playing with toys, etc.) works well. A "lesson" on the signs *eat*, *more*, and *all done* fits naturally into mealtime. Similarly, signs for *bath*, *water*, and *toys* are easily incorporated into your bath time routine.

A baby's attention gravitates toward the newest, loudest, and most energetic thing in the room. Unlike adults, babies cannot selectively engage in one activity and block out background activities. Signing lessons cannot compete with loud noises and rapid movements, so minimize distractions in your environment. Switch off the TV and put away toys that are not currently in use. Also, let family members know that signing time is not an appropriate time for them to engage in boisterous or distracting activities.

Minimize background distractions.

Motivated Signing

Learning sign language is more enjoyable when signs are linked to fun things. The first few signs should represent items or activities that Baby enjoys and is motivated to learn. Labeling a source of entertainment or fascination makes Baby happy. *Bath*, *dog*, *cat*, and *fan* are fun signs that are frequently encountered by Baby.

Signs that help Baby communicate his needs are also motivating. Consequently, these signs are learned faster. For example, signs for *milk*, *food*, *mom*, *dad*, and *up* (as in "pick me up") are popular initial signs.

Integrating signs into fun activities also increases Baby's motivation to sign. For example, signing while you read a book motivates Baby to learn the signs so he can join in.

Repetition

Repetition is the secret to Baby Sign Language success. Frequent exposure to signing ensures signs will stick in your baby's memory. Consider how many times a child hears a word before he starts saying it. Just as repetition of spoken words leads to learning, lots of repetition with signing gestures is necessary to learn sign language.

Combine repetition with a pinch of fun and a dash of encouragement and you have the recipe for successfully teaching your child Baby Sign Language.

How Can Children in Deaf Families Sign at Six Months?

Children born in deaf families sign as early as six months old. How can these babies sign so early?

Children in deaf families are constantly exposed to signing. Their parents are not only signing to Baby, but to their spouse, other children, and friends. With all this exposure to signing, it is inevitable that a baby quickly starts signing.

Timing: Before, During, and After

There are three opportunities for signing a word: before, during, and after the event. When giving your baby milk, you can make the sign *milk* while you are preparing to feed him, while he is feeding, and immediately after he finishes.

The best time to sign is the moment before an object or action is presented. Studies of learning suggest this is the optimal time to

Signing before, during, and after.

create an association between the sign and the meaning.

Signing during an event or while an object is at the center of Baby's attention is also effective (and a little easier to time). For example, repeatedly sign *eat* when Baby is eating. If your baby is fixated on the family cat, sign *cat*. Signing during an event tends to happen naturally.

Finally, you can make the sign immediately after the object is presented or the action has occurred.

Particularly in the early phase of signing, repeat a sign many times in succession. Remember that repetition is the key to success. Have we repeated that enough yet?

Daily Routines

Create signing routines and rituals, especially when you are just getting started. Children love repetition, which is why they like to listen to the same songs, read the same books, and watch the same movies over and over again. Familiarity instills confidence and a sense of control over their environment. You can take advantage of this drive for familiarity by incorporating signs into their daily rituals.

Meals and bedtimes are opportunities to incorporate signing in routine activities. When giving your baby cereal in the morning, give him a small amount, let him finish, then sign *more*. Give him a second small serving, let him finish, then sign *more* again before handing out the next serving.

You can even establish mini-routines. For example, sign *up* before lifting your baby into your arms. Sign *sleep* before you put him down for the night. Sign *bath* before you start his bath and *car* before you load him into the car. Signing *goodbye* as visitors leave allows guests to become involved in signing practice.

Routines create ample opportunities for signing practice and don't require you to find time for dedicated signing lessons.

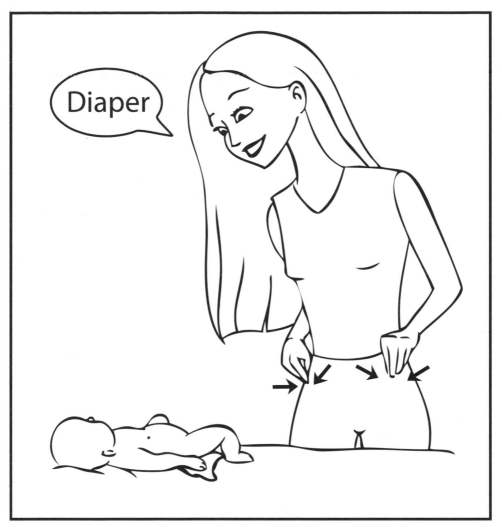

*Everyday routines, like changing a diaper,
are ideal opportunities to practice signs.*

Creating Opportunities

Advanced signs are those that are infrequently used as part of your day-to-day routine. After all, who sees an elephant or a bear every day? To teach these advanced signs, you must create opportunities for routine exposure. Picture books, songs, and flash cards are a great way to create these opportunities.

Picture Books

Books are one of the best tools to create signing opportunities. As part of storytelling, incorporate the relevant signs. Babies love hearing the same books again and again, which creates numerous signing opportunities.

When possible, choose simple picture books featuring the words you are teaching. We recommend, particularly for children younger than 18 months, simple books where each page has one clear theme. For example, *One Boy*, (by Laura Vaccaro Seeger) presents the numbers 1-10. For more detailed information on using books, see *Chapter 5: Advanced Teaching Methods*.

Videos

Short videos can be used to show Baby many things he is unlikely to encounter in everyday life. Let Baby's interests guide you. If Baby is interested in machines, then watch clips of tractors. If Baby is interested in people, show him videos of family members.

Wildlife videos are a popular choice. Watching a *lion* roar, or a *dolphin* play in the sea is a great way to learn signs and pass the time on rainy days. YouTube (www.youtube.com) is a great source of free videos on almost any topic.

Songs

Songs are an entertaining way to practice signing. Simply take a classic song and choose a few signs that apply to the verse or chorus. Songs that follow a single theme are easiest to learn. For example, *Old MacDonald Had a Farm* is a wonderful song for signing because animal signs can be repeated throughout the song.

Flash Cards

Flash cards are a terrific tool for teaching Baby Sign Language. Select five cards to start, then add cards to your deck as Baby masters the initial series of signs. Signing familiar words boosts confidence while Baby learns new signs. Intersperse new words into the game so that Baby does not take on all new words at once. This intermingling approach bolsters Baby's confidence and helps Baby maintain focus. Teaching Baby too many new signs at once is overwhelming, so progress gradually. For additional information on using flash cards and other teaching aids, see *Chapter 5*.

Reviewing Early Signs

As you continue to add new signs, remember to revisit less frequently used signs. Use the worksheet at the end of the book to track the signs your baby has learned. Periodically review the list and create opportunities to use all of the signs. Revisiting past lessons is integral to maintaining a robust sign language vocabulary. Periodic reviews are also opportunities to observe and celebrate progress.

Baby-Initiated Signs

Baby-initiated signs happen when a baby makes a sign without being prompted. As your baby begins to sign, more practice opportunities will come from baby-initiated signs. When Baby initiates a sign, sign back and say the word. If he has made a request, like *water*, acknowledge the request verbally and fulfill the request when possible.

Baby-initiated signing provides insight into which words Baby finds interesting and which words Baby has learned. Use this information to help you select words Baby will be most motivated to learn.

Modeling Signs

Whether it is a toddler putting his hands on his hips or a child putting on his father's shoes, children are supreme imitators.

Children place importance on the behavior of parents and siblings and therefore learn many behaviors by simply emulating what they observe. Accordingly, some of the best exposure to signing comes from family members signing to one another. If you sign to one another, your baby will learn from that interaction just as powerfully as if you were signing to him directly. Incorporate some basic signs into your interactions with other adults and older children. Some ASL basics like, *mom*, *dad*, *sister*, *brother*, *eat*, *more*, and *drink* are easy and add a bit of fun to family life.

We delve further into modeling techniques in *Chapter 6* as we explain the Pepperberg Method.

Encouragement

The time invested to teach and incorporate signs into your life will pay off as your child starts to sign back. Nurture these initial sparks of signing with plenty of calm encouragement. Encouragement provides motivation for further signing development.

Several months may pass before your child responds with a sign. Stick with it. Do not give up. With consistent exposure, your baby WILL sign and it will be fabulous! It is up to you as the coach to stay determined.

Less is More:
Insights from Washoe

The trainers of Washoe (one of the first chimpanzees to be taught sign language) learned a valuable lesson about using rewards. When they began teaching Washoe, his trainers used rewards such as tickling and food to encourage development.

continued

Initial progress was slow as Washoe learned only individual words.

Eventually, Washoe's trainers realized that the rewards were interfering with the learning process. For example, tickling Washoe and giving him treats got him excited and became an impediment to learning (i.e., overstimulation). The trainers also discovered that Washoe was just performing the signs for treats and was not trying to communicate.

Washoe's trainers achieved more success when they focused on demonstrating signs and interacting with Washoe. These interactions provided Washoe an opportunity to use signs to communicate. Washoe learned significantly more by observing and imitating, with the ultimate reward being the ability to communicate with his trainers. The fulfillment experienced by being able to communicate was much more motivating than any treats or praise.

Encouragement is good, but the real reward is the ability to communicate. For babies, just knowing that you understand them is enough.

Recognition

Baby's first signs are usually rough approximations of the actual signs. Babies lack the muscle control, particularly the fine muscle control, that adults take for granted. Young children often have difficulty moving individual fingers and positioning their hands. Babies are also new to signing and have not yet learned exactly where everything needs to go. These two factors combine for some wacky signs. For example, instead of perfectly motioning the sign for *mom* or *dad,* you will often see Baby flailing his hands. This makes initial signs easy to miss.

Initial attempts are rough approximations of the true sign.

Recognize the challenges your child faces with his first signs and keep a close watch for motions that resemble signs. In particular, be aware of any subtle arm movements when you are signing to Baby or when Baby is exposed to something that corresponds to a sign you have been working on. A few things to watch for include:

Delay

After exposure to a sign, babies often wait up to 60 seconds before imitating. Give your child plenty of time to mirror your motions. Your baby is studying your movements and trying to make his uncooperative body do what he wants. Don't forget, it takes time to adjust to a new body!

Gross Motor Skills

Expect the first signs to use motions that involve gross motor skills (e.g., arm movements). Elements of signs requiring fine motor skills, such as finger positioning, will come later.

Concentration and Release

Before your baby forms a sign you will often see a look of intense concentration on his face. After making the sign, he may also break into a self-congratulatory smile, which is one of those moments that makes Baby Sign Language especially fulfilling. So be patient if you observe a concentrated visage, a sign may be about to follow.

Repetition

Babies repeat the signs they learn as if they are playing a game. They will naturally repeat a sign in an attempt to learn the sign, much the same way a child will repeat the same word over and over again when learning to speak.

If your child's motions resemble a sign, immediately offer encouragement. Don't worry about false alarms. Even if your baby is not trying to sign, encouraging him when he is motioning will facilitate sign development.

Calm Encouragement

Encouragement is good. Calm encouragement is better. Praise helps your baby understand that he is progressing and shows him that signing is important. Praise is also crucial to keep signing fun for your baby.

Remember to give Baby energetic praise, not hyper-energetic praise. Attention and responsiveness will suffice in most situations. For most children, just knowing that their motions are interpreted correctly provides all the encouragement they need.

Because the definition of "calm encouragement" varies substantially among parents, here are a few tips:

Acknowledgment

Any time your baby motions a sign, acknowledge his effort to communicate. Repeat the sign back to Baby and say the corresponding word. The simple act of repeating the sign lets Baby know you understand his sign and that you are attentive to his signing. This acknowledgment is the most effective encouragement you can offer.

For example, if your baby signs *dog* when he sees a dog on a walk, acknowledge the sign by saying the word and making the sign back. "Yes, it is a *dog*."

If Baby is deliberately signing and you are unsure what sign he is forming, still acknowledge the attempt. You can try and guess by asking "Did you see a *dog*?" while making the appropriate sign. Or, if you have no idea, simply say "I'm not sure what you are saying, can you make the sign again?" Correct interpretation is not as important as rewarding Baby's attempt to communicate, and the best reward is your attention.

Emotion

Excitement is natural when your baby is learning to sign. Focus this energy and be expressive, showing Baby that you are happy he is signing. Make exaggerated motions to show Baby how you appreciate his effort.

Gratification

Beyond acknowledgment and emotion, show Baby that you understand what is being communicated by giving Baby what he wants. Learning that signs can help Baby get what he wants and exert some control over his surroundings is a powerful motivator to continue signing.

Encourage Baby by acknowledging the sign,
displaying positive emotion, and responding to the sign.

If your baby signs to *eat* or *drink*, acknowledge the communication by saying the word and signing back. Then, when possible, accommodate the request. There are of course limits, but particularly when Baby is starting out, try and fulfill his request.

If you cannot meet the request, at least acknowledge the sign. It is sometimes tempting to pretend not to understand or to ignore a sign. But, remember that while not getting what he wants is frustrating to Baby, not being understood is even more frustrating. Always acknowledge the sign and show that you understand. For example, in turning down a signed request to go to the park you might say "You want to go to the *park*?" "I'm afraid we can't go to the *park* today." Baby may still fuss if he does not get his way, but the frustration is less when he knows he is understood.

Forget Perfection

Signs are not formed perfectly the first time. For that matter, signs may not be formed perfectly after the first hundred times. Baby's early signs will be approximations of the actual signs. Regardless, keep up the encouragement. Initial signs will get better every week. Progress may seem imperceptible, but it is happening. If you keep using the sign, your baby will continue to improve. Practice makes perfect!

Expansion

Once your baby is confidently using his first few signs, it is time to increase your signing vocabulary. More words offer new development opportunities and expand Baby's ability to communicate. Add words that help Baby day-to-day, help advance his education, or that relate to your baby's interests.

When expanding Baby's vocabulary we want to strike a balance between keeping Baby challenged and overwhelming Baby with too many new signs.

Incremental Expansion

Learning requires gradual progression, so focus on a few new signs at a time. Introducing too much new material at one time can be overwhelming for your child. Select a few new signs and provide lots of exposure to the new signs until they are learned. As Baby grasps the new words, slowly add a few more signs.

After learning the first five signs, work on only two to three new signs at any one time. As your baby becomes more advanced, you can add larger sets (5-10) of new signs.

Categories to Specifics

In the early phase of signing, "category" signs are used to encompass many specific but related items. For example, *eat* initially refers to anything and everything your baby eats. As Baby's signing progresses, you can introduce more specific words like *cracker* (referring to all cracker-like snacks, such as pretzels, chips, etc.), and *juice* (referring to drinks that are not milk, water, or soda). Similarly, you can become even more specific and use compound signs like *orange juice* or *animal cracker*. You can also incorporate descriptors like *big cup* and *little cup*, or *yellow cup* and *blue cup*.

The transition from categories to specifics will happen across Baby's vocabulary. Other categories that can be further specified include

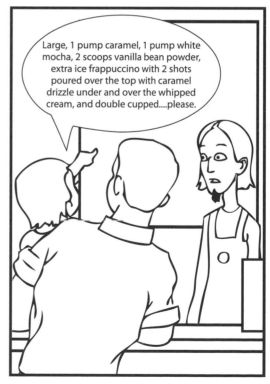

Encourage Baby to make requests more specific.

clothes (going from *shirt*, to *flower shirt*), animals (going from *bug* to *ant*), vehicles (going from *car* to *truck*), and toys (going from *blocks* to *big blocks*).

Difficulty of Signs

Begin by teaching Baby only easy words. Gradually increase the level of difficulty as Baby becomes more adept at signing and his linguistic abilities improve.

Everyday Simple Words

The easiest signs to teach are those representing everyday items and events in your baby's life. For example, signs representing everyday people and pets such as *mom*, *dad*, *cat*, and *dog* are easy for your baby to grasp. Objects such as *ball*, *fan*, *book*, *phone*, and *car* are also easily learned. Other signs in this category include common foods such as *milk*, *water*, and *rice*, and everyday events like *bath*, *bye-bye*, *up* (for pick me up) and *good-night*. Because Baby observes these signs often and the meanings are straightforward, these words represent great starter signs.

Occasional Simple Words

After everyday words, begin introducing simple words that are not as common in Baby's life, but are compelling to him. Great words in this category include animals such as *tiger*, *duck*, and *horse*, or transportation signs like *boat*, *bus*, and *train*. This second group of signs is often introduced using flash cards, videos, or other media because they do not occur frequently in a baby's routine.

Descriptive Words

Finally, incorporate words that describe size, color, and number. This category includes words such as *big*, *purple*, and *seven*. These descriptive words are typically combined with simple nouns (e.g., *big dog*). We further explore compounding in *Chapter 8*.

Signing Themes

Once Baby masters the basics, begin to center your teaching sessions on themes. Teaching multiple signs along a theme is an extremely effective coaching technique as the baby learns by comparison. Cycle through signs clustered around a theme, and let Baby sign each item in turn. Food is a topic of importance to Baby, so introduce signs like *milk, water, bread, fruit,* and whatever else Baby likes to eat. Animals are always popular, making it easy to teach everything from *cat* and *dog,* to the more exotic *elephant* and *giraffe.* Colors like *red, blue,* and *green* are perennial favorites as well.

Numbers are also a good theme, but best taught to older or more advanced signers. You can begin by teaching Baby to count from *one* to *five* by signing. Then graduate to combining number signs with simple noun signs (e.g., *three cups*).

Curiosity Driven Signs

A child's curiosity is a powerful tool to utilize when introducing new signs. When your baby is curious about something, quickly introduce the sign and the word to satisfy that curiosity.

Older children can learn the verb *sign* (see illustration on page 60), which becomes your prompt to provide the sign for any new situation or object.

Try to anticipate new words. If you are going to the zoo, practice your animal signs. You may also print a few flash cards to take along for reference. Of course no one can anticipate all new signs that you may want to use. So if you don't know the exact sign, look up the sign, approximate the sign, or invent your own "home sign".

Sign: used to ask for the sign for a word.

Look Up the Sign

When near a computer or smartphone with internet access you can quickly find the sign you need. We are partial to our online dictionary at www.BabySignLanguage.com/dictionary. There are also American Sign Language dictionaries at www.lifeprint.com and www.ASLpro.com. Whatever your resource, finding the sign will ensure you are teaching your child the correct ASL version.

As with spoken languages, there are variations within the American Sign Language community. Different people will sometimes form the sign for the same word differently. This is just a matter of preference. It is not important which variation of a sign you use as long as you use the same variation every time.

Approximate

If a reference guide is not available, approximations will suffice. For example, if your baby sees a zebra at the zoo and wants to know the sign, you can use the sign *horse*. Of course this is not perfectly correct, but the primary purpose of Baby Sign Language is to help your baby communicate. The conversation surrounding an approximate sign might go something like this: "That animal is a zebra. A zebra is like a *horse*." Once you return home you can look up the sign for zebra. Find a picture of a zebra, teach Baby the sign, and revisit the topic by saying, "This is a *zebra*. Do you remember the *zebra* at the zoo? A *zebra* is like a *horse*."

Home Signs

As a last resort, create your own signs. Improvised signs are okay, but make sure to jot them down. Otherwise, you might find yourself forgetting your own signs!

Chapter Three
Five Stages of Signing Development

This chapter takes you through the stages of learning Baby Sign Language. While each child's development trajectory is unique, the following five stages of learning are typical:

1. **Recognition** - Baby appreciates that signs are significant and pays particular attention to your signing

2. **Imitation** - Baby imitates signs that she observes someone else making

3. **Understanding** - Baby understands the meaning of signs

4. **Initiation** - Baby makes a sign without prompting in order to initiate communication

5. **Combination** - Baby joins two or more signs to create phrases

As babies start learning sign language, they typically pass through five stages: recognition, imitation, understanding, initiation, and combination. Understanding this pattern of development helps you monitor progress, diagnose challenges, and determine where coaching is needed.

Of course children may follow different development trajectories. Some children will progress faster, and some children will progress slower. And sometimes, the steps may be a little out of order. Each child will have her own pace and sequence, so don't worry if she does not stringently follow the five stages.

Late Start, Strong Finish

We started signing to my daughter when she was 12 months old and we were initially concerned that it might be too late to start. She is now 21 months and uses well over 200 signs.

In the past few months she has started talking, so she doesn't need signs as much to communicate. But, it is a habit for her to use the signs while saying the words. She speaks 500-600 words now and I believe sign language was a major help!

Meghan Kilpatrick

Stage 1: Recognition

Signing begins with recognition. Recognition means your baby will begin to realize that signs are important and are used to communicate. Although your baby may not comprehend the meaning, she recognizes that something significant is happening.

Recognition may occur within the first few weeks. An early milestone is reached when your baby focuses on your hands instead of your face. This usually involves a contemplative look followed by a pause.

Remember, when your baby watches you motion a sign, reward her with your full attention, a pause, a repeat of the sign, and a smile.

Recognition: Baby's eyes follow your hands.

Stage 2: Imitation

Once recognition is achieved, the next step is imitation. As all parents know, babies love to copy grown-ups. You have probably seen a toddler hold a phone to her ear just like a grown-up. In much the same way, your Baby will copy your signing hand motions. Although she does not grasp the meaning of each motion, she wants to copy your behavior. Initiation of signs is unlikely during the imitation stage. Therefore, Baby will wait until you sign, then attempt to make the same sign back.

The return sign will often be delayed several seconds, so be patient. Baby will watch you form the sign, furrow her brow as she tries to figure out how to use her hands, then produce a tentative sign.

During the imitation stage, signs will often be rough approximations of the technically correct signs. As always, encourage all attempts at signing with enthusiasm by repeating the sign and pausing to allow a return sign. Playing the copycat game is your baby's reward.

Imitation: Baby mimics your signing motions.

Stage 3: Understanding

In the third stage of signing development, Baby starts to understand what a sign means. She will anticipate actions associated with the sign and modify her actions accordingly. For example, if you sign *milk*, Baby will become excited and start clawing at your shirt or grabbing for her bottle as well as signing back.

Once your baby starts to understand the signs, remember to pause and allow her time to sign back. Often in our excitement we rush to give Baby what she wants, but this denies her the opportunity to communicate. Allowing time for a return sign facilitates the next stage of development when she starts to initiate signs.

Note that the order of the imitation stage and the understanding stage are often reversed.

Understanding: Baby comprehends the meaning of your sign.

Stage 4: Initiation

In the fourth phase of learning, Baby will initiate communication using signs. Typically these initial signs relate to food or something important in their environment. Sometimes babies make signs simply as a way of processing what they are thinking.

In the latter part of the initiation stage, Baby will start generalizing signs. The sign *dog* might now refer to not only your own pet, but the neighbor's dog, or a dog in a book.

The best way to reward signing at this stage is to acknowledge that you understand your baby by signing back and repeating the word. If practical and appropriate, gratify requests by giving your baby what she wants.

Once Baby has initiated a few signs, it is time to start expanding her vocabulary.

Initiation: Baby initiates the sign without prompting.

Stage 5: Combination

The final stage of signing development involves your baby forming phrases with her signs. In this stage, babies will combine two or more signs to convey more complex thoughts. For example, instead of just signing *up*, Baby might sign *daddy up* to specify that she wants daddy to hold her.

Baby Sentences

My 12 month old daughter, Livi, keeps forming more elaborate sign "sentences" requesting cookies. This weekend she signed "*PLEASE, PLEASE, PLEASE eat cookies!*"

Jody Anderson Dragon

Combining signs is an advanced skill usually performed by experienced baby signers. Combining signs is fun for adults because babies come up with creative word combinations as they try and make sense of the world around them. For example, a hair dryer might be a *fan hot*.

Encourage combination signing by modeling the behavior and combining signs where you previously only used a single sign. For example, instead of just pointing out a *dog*, you might use *big dog* or *little dog*. Or instead of picking the *flower*, you might pick the *blue flower*.

We explore this topic in greater detail in *Chapter 6* when we discuss *Signing Phrases*.

Combination: Baby begins combining signs to make phrases.
(Baby is signing "ball" "red")

Chapter Four
Getting Everyone Involved

Involving a spouse, family member, or friend in Baby Sign Language creates more opportunities for exposure. This chapter explores ways to involve others, including:

- **Siblings** - use peer influence and get Baby's brothers and sisters in on the act

- **Grandparents** - show grandma and grandpa fun ways they can bond with their precious grandchild

- **Caregivers & Schools** - work with Baby's teachers to create more sign language exposure

- **Friends** - teach friends a few signs to use around your baby

- **Naysayers** - defuse the occasional signing humbug

Sign language is more compelling to Baby when she receives signs from several people. The more you incorporate signing into family life, the faster your baby will progress with signing. Babies learn by observing and copying. When your baby sees other people signing, she becomes even more motivated to learn. This is particularly true of older siblings. As the saying goes, "it takes a village to raise a child" (or more appropriately, "monkey see – monkey do").

In our experience, family members and friends become curious when they see Baby Sign Language in action. They want to learn a few signs so they too can communicate with Baby. Nobody wants to miss out on the fun.

Many baby/toddler classes, activities, and care facilities already incorporate signing into their programs. Use this collective enthusiasm for signing to get everyone involved.

Big Sister Helps Out

We taught BSL to our older daughter Lorelei as a baby, and then when we found out that her little sister Lily was deaf, we continued signing. When Lily was 9 months old, 3 year old Lorelei walked up to her and moved Lily's hand to sign *mommy*, then pointed to me and called me mommy. Lily, who has cerebral palsy and a lot of physical limitations, has been signing *mommy* ever since.

Danielle Bennett

Siblings and Grandparents

Older Siblings

There is no greater influence for learning Baby Sign Language than a committed family member. Older siblings love the responsibility of teaching younger siblings how to sign, and babies love to imitate older brothers and sisters. Take advantage of this situation by encouraging siblings to sign to their baby brother or sister.

Older children will happily play signing games with the new baby as this allows them to interact with him and play the role of grown-up. Sibling signing is also a way for older children to bond with the newest member of the family. Instead of competing for attention, older brothers or sisters focus on teaching Baby. To facilitate the process, reward both the baby and the older sibling with your attention.

Older siblings love helping Baby sign.

If you have older children who learned to sign, they can immediately start teaching Baby the signs they learned.

If your older children did not learn sign language, you can still recruit them to be Baby Sign Language teachers; you just need to help them learn the signs. Stoke their enthusiasm by allowing them to teach you. Ask them from time to time to remind you of signs you have "forgotten." To help them learn, let them peruse our online dictionary (www.BabySignLanguage.com/dictionary).

Grandparents

Most grandparents, although they may have heard of Baby Sign Language, know little about the topic and have never signed to communicate. However, grandparents adore their grandchildren and are eager to bond with their beloved grandbabies. The best way to get grandparents hooked is to teach them a handful of signs, then watch their eyes light up when Baby starts signing to them. Grandparents will then be highly motivated to expand their vocabulary and will expect you to be their signing tutor. If they are internet savvy, direct them to our website. Alternatively,

Teaching Grandson

My oldest grandson will be nine months old in a few days and I take care of him two days a week. I started by signing *food* and *milk* when it comes time to feed him. Now that he has learned those signs, I have started adding more signs like *more* and *all done*.

Laura Skinner

loan them a copy of this book to help them learn. Grandparents who have seen Baby Sign Language in action are some of the biggest enthusiasts in the signing community.

When involving grandparents, be sure to coordinate your signs. Grandparents should use the same set of signs you use. Ask grandparents to let you know when they introduce new signs. This ensures that you are prepared if Baby makes a new sign he learned from his grandparents. It also allows you to practice the new signs with your child, which ensures he will remember the signs when grandparents next visit.

At-Home Caregivers

Due to the growing popularity of Baby Sign Language, many professional caregivers already know how to sign. Those unable to sign should be eager to learn Baby Sign Language as it makes their job a lot easier and more fun.

A great way to help caregivers learn is to provide a Baby Sign Language wall chart (www.BabySignLanguage.com/chart) or a set of flash cards (www.BabySignLanguage.com/flash-cards) in your home. As you add signs, keep your caregiver informed so they learn the new signs.

Involving your baby's caregiver creates continuity and reinforcement throughout the day. This also mitigates any frustration for both the baby and caregiver if Baby is trying to communicate through signs and the caregiver cannot understand.

With temporary caregivers like babysitters, just give them a crash course in the most commonly used signs (e.g., *eat, drink, sleep*) and refer them to the wall chart.

*Show babysitters a signing wall chart
to help them recognize basic signs.*

Daycare, Preschool, and Classes

Many daycares, preschools, and baby classes incorporate signing into their curriculum to aid cognitive development and improve speech skills. Being surrounded by other signing children creates a wonderful learning environment. This immersion into signing accelerates signing development.

As a side benefit, it is a thrill to see two young children communicate via sign language. You haven't seen cute until you see one baby signing to another baby!

If your daycare does not offer signing, suggest it to your child's teacher. Most educators have heard of Baby Sign Language and are open to giving it a try. Introducing a bit of signing during song time is an easy and fun way for children to start learning a few basic signs.

Friends

Teach your friends a few signs they can use to interact with your baby. Involving friends will help them develop a stronger connection with your child.

Forming signing groups with other parents of similarly aged children is a good way to engage your friends and their children in a developmental activity. Signing groups also facilitate friendships among adults. Arrange play dates to incorporate a bit of signing into your activities. If you already belong to a non-signing play group, suggest signing to the other parents; they may already be signing at home or at least considering it.

Naysayers

You may have the misfortune of encountering someone that is not supportive of Baby Sign Language. Some people just do not like anything new or different. Some naysayers are misinformed, and others are just pessimists.

There is nothing to be gained by engaging with people that are negative about Baby Sign Language. They will likely offer plenty of excuses to do nothing and you will not change their mind by arguing with them.

Instead, keep signing. Soon you and your baby will be communicating and the naysayers will have nothing left to say. They can either jump on the bandwagon or miss out on the fun.

Three Months Later

Naysayers quickly change their tune
once they see results for themselves.

Grandma Melts

My mother-in-law thought Baby Sign Language was crazy until she came to visit in May and saw how Frances responded to her signs. She nearly melted when I signed *grandma* and Baby smiled at it. I've since put a picture of grandma on the flash card and hung it up.

Angela Hortman

Chapter Five
Advanced Teaching Methods

Beyond the basic teaching methods, we explore new ways to keep Baby engaged and stimulated, including:

- **Flash Cards** - use flash cards to jumpstart and broaden learning

- **Props** - incorporate figurines, dolls, and household items into signing practice

- **Books** - sign along to Baby's favorite picture books to make story time more engaging and educational

- **Pepperberg Method** - work with a partner to model signs

As your baby progresses in her signing, begin using advanced teaching methods to add a bit of variety to signing lessons. Advanced teaching methods enhance the learning experience and stimulate development by engaging your child in different ways.

Flash Cards

Flash cards are an excellent tool for expanding your child's vocabulary beyond everyday words. Flash cards provide visuals of objects that are infrequently experienced in real life, such as lion, beach, and airplane. Flash cards also create opportunities to reinforce signs that Baby has already learned.

Turn flash cards into a game with your little one. Most babies love playing with their cards and will often bring you the flash cards to initiate a game. Theme-based flash card sessions are great for teaching animals, numbers, or colors. Flash cards are also useful for keeping your baby occupied outside the home (e.g., long car rides, waiting for a table at a restaurant, at the doctor's office).

When introducing flash cards, select five cards representing signs your baby already knows. As your baby masters these flash cards, add cards of unfamiliar signs. Before long, Baby will be able to sign the entire deck. Baby Sign Language flash cards are available on our site. You can also make your own by printing out the flash cards from our website and attaching them to cardboard (www.BabySignLanguage.com/flash-cards).

As your child masters the initial set of flash cards, add to the fun and development by asking questions about the flash cards. If the flash card represents a monkey, ask "What sound does a *monkey* make?" Ask Baby to identify body parts. "Point to the *monkey*'s nose." "Point to the *monkey*'s feet." And ask Baby about colors. "What color is the *monkey*?"

For color flash cards, ask the child to find other objects of the same color. "What else is *blue*?" "Can you point to something else that is *red*?"

For number flash cards, ask the baby to count up to that number (using signs). "Can you count to *four*?" Or ask them to bring you that number of some conveniently located objects. "Can you bring me *four* blocks?"

You can even teach older children to finger spell the words on the flash cards to develop reading and spelling skills. Be creative with flash cards and come up with a system that is engaging and educational for your baby.

Keep sessions short and end flash card time when you sense that Baby's enthusiasm is waning. This will ensure your baby perceives flash cards as a treat and will remain enthusiastic about playing with the cards.

Flash cards help teach less common words
and improve understanding.

Props

Similar to flash cards, props can be used to make sign language lessons more engaging. For the kinesthetic or active child, the ability to touch and hold toys representing each new sign facilitates learning while adding to the enjoyment of the lesson. When possible, organize props around a single theme such as animals, colors, numbers, or actions. Theme-inspired props help your child learn by allowing him to compare similar items. This helps you avoid overwhelming your child with too many new ideas in a single session. The following are examples of props to use when teaching a collection of signs around a specific theme.

Figurines and Dolls

Most children are interested in animals. Animal figurines are widely available and represent a perfect theme-based collection of props.

Dolls or action figures with moveable arms and legs are great props for teaching action signs like *jump* and *lie down*. Mimicking actions and teaching the corresponding signs is much easier with a doll than with a flash card.

You can also use figurines and dolls to teach parts of the body. For example, teaching the sign for *mouth* with Baby's own mouth, the mouth of a doll, and the mouth of an animal figurine helps Baby generalize the concept of mouth. Taking knowledge from one context and applying it to another context is an important part of Baby's development.

Blocks

The classic painted wooden blocks are perfect props to teach colors, letters, and numbers. Blocks can also be utilized for adjectives such as *tall*, *short*, *close*, and *far*. Too many blocks within Baby's reach are distracting, so use only a few blocks when teaching signs. Blocks are available at most toy stores, but can also be easily improvised with small boxes (e.g., single-serve cereal boxes).

Electronic Toys

Electronic toys bring another helpful element to the learning experience. Toys that play music and that have a volume control can help the child learn *loud* and *quiet*. Electronic toys are also excellent for teaching the signs *on* and *off*.

Household Items

Household items can also be used to help teach signing. There is no need to purchase anything, just use a little creativity and the objects already in your home. As an added bonus, using household objects makes it easier to integrate signing into your everyday routine.

Switches

Switches for ceiling fans, lamps, and lights provide plenty of entertainment as Baby learns to turn the light *on* and *off*. Household switches are also fun for your child as they are simple to use and provide instant gratification.

Containers

Plastic food storage containers are an excellent teaching resource. As a bonus, they can occupy Baby while you are working in the kitchen. Containers facilitate the teaching of concepts such as:

In and Out: put the pretzel *in* the container, then take it *out*.

Off and On: put the lid *on*, then take it *off*.

Open and Close: *open* the container and then *close* the container.

Clothes

Some children simply do not enjoy changing clothes or getting dressed. As with most activities children dislike, getting dressed means being forced to do something against their will. Empowerment is crucial, so try this fun activity to get them feeling more involved in the process while also teaching clothing signs.

Put clothes on a favorite doll and sign along.

Choose a doll or stuffed animal that is approximately the size of a newborn. Select several items of newborn clothing that you lovingly packed away. If you still have some tiny diapers lying around, gather those too.

Dress the doll or stuffed animal with your baby. Let your baby do as much as she can when dressing the doll. This will show your baby that getting dressed can be enjoyable. Never miss a learning opportunity, so teach the signs for each piece of clothing as you go.

Baby should be less resistant to changing clothes or being dressed once she has dressed her own baby doll and can sign along to each piece of clothing.

Stuffed Animals

Toddlers love to feed stuffed animals. The action does not stop there as they also want to sit them on the potty, put them in the stroller, take a nap with them, etc.

Take advantage of this connection by incorporating stuffed animals into signing sessions. For example, ask Baby to give Teddy something to *eat*. Or, ask her to teach Teddy the sign for *potty*.

Again, be creative with the items already in your home. Opportunities to teach and practice Baby Sign Language are everywhere!

Books

Incorporating sign language into story time is a fantastic way to engage your child in both Baby Sign Language and reading. Sign along to your favorite books by selecting one sign for each page, then make the sign as you read the word. Once she is capable, let your baby sign along or even initiate the signs.

Signing along to a book works particularly well with simple picture books like Bill Martin's classic *Brown Bear, Brown Bear*, which has a clear theme for each page. The first page is about a bear, followed by a page about a bird, followed by a page about a duck, etc. When your baby is 18 months or younger, spend more time with these simple one-idea-per-page books. More complex books are entertaining for older children, but tend to confuse younger ones.

Simple books with a single idea on each page are best.

Books are particularly great learning resources because they provide many opportunities for signing repetition. Children love to hear the same story again and again, so use these opportunities for signing development. And since children love when a book is read to them, signing along is fun. As with flash cards, you can extend the signing lesson with questions as your child gets older. For example, ask them the color of the bear, or the sound a duck makes, or how many birds they see.

Pepperberg Method

The Pepperberg Method is one of our favorite teaching tools for babies 12 to 18 months old. This method is effective for teaching numerous signs quickly and is based on the idea of peer learning.

The traditional teaching techniques discussed up to this point involve signing directly to your baby. The Pepperberg method involves peer modeling. This method adds a third person to the signing session. The third person will be your coaching partner and will help model signs for your baby.

We named this method after Professor Irene Pepperberg. For more information on her work, see the box on page 90.

How to Use the Pepperberg Method

Two signers (instructor and responder) are required to perform the Pepperberg Method. This can be you and another adult or you and an older child. Place yourselves in a triangle where all three participants (instructor, responder, and baby) can clearly view the other participants. Sitting around a dining table works well. Be sure to have a bowl of your baby's favorite snack on hand. We use crackers in our example.

First, the instructor asks the responder if he wants a cracker while making the *cracker* sign to the responder. The responder replies "cracker" and makes the sign back to the instructor. Once the responder correctly signs *cracker*, the instructor gives the responder a cracker. You will notice Baby keenly observing the interaction, with her eyes fixing on the instructor, shifting to the responder, then back to the instructor.

*Pepperberg Method: Model the act of signing
and show the reward for signing.*

Once the responder receives the snack, the instructor then offers another delectable treat to the baby. The first few times the baby is offered the snack, she may jump out of her highchair with excitement trying to snag the cracker. Howls of protest may also accompany this excitement if the baby does not receive the cracker. Remember, this is all to be expected as the baby is initially exposed to the Pepperberg Method. Calmly ignore anything that is not the sign for *cracker*.

If the baby makes any approximation of the sign, then give her the cracker. As mentioned before, we are not looking for perfection, only progress. However, if Baby does not make any signing movements, return your attention to the responder and repeat the exercise.

By modeling the desired behavior and using peer influence, the Pepperberg Method significantly accelerates signing development. This method is particularly useful when teaching food signs, but can also be employed using small props like animal figurines or wooden blocks.

Irene Pepperberg and Alex the Parrot

Irene Pepperberg (now Professor Pepperberg) was a graduate student at Harvard when she set out to teach a parrot to talk. (Now you know why we used crackers in our example!) Although parrots had been trained to mimic human speech for centuries, Pepperberg

continued

wanted to know if parrots could talk as a way of communicating. Before Pepperberg, no one had successfully taught a bird to communicate in any real sense.

When teaching a parrot to speak, most researchers and pet owners stood in front of the parrot, showed them an object, and then repeated the word for the object. Results were disappointing with this technique and limited to vocal mimicry. Therefore, it was widely (but wrongly) assumed that birds were not smart enough to communicate by speaking.

Pepperberg, with the help of her parrot Alex, tried something different – an approach called "model/rival." The "model/rival" method involves two trainers. One trainer provides instructions and the other trainer models the appropriate behavior. The "rival" component of the technique is derived from the observation that animals in the wild learn by watching and studying other animals. By observing role models, animals are able to learn more effectively.

Remarkably, Alex developed a 150 word vocabulary and was able to communicate, albeit in a rudimentary way. Alex could count, perform basic arithmetic, and answer simple questions. Not only had Irene Pepperberg proven the benefits of the "model/rival" method, but Alex became quite the popular figure. When Alex passed away in 2007 at the age of 31, he was widely mourned and received an obituary in the New York Times. Not bad for a pet store parrot that most people considered too dumb to talk!

Informal Pepperberg Method

Although the Pepperberg Method is a structured technique for learning that requires a dedicated coaching session, the concept of modeling signs can be incorporated into daily routines.

The best way to incorporate modeling is to sign with other family members. When you ask your partner to pass a book, use the *book* sign and have them repeat the sign back to you. When you instruct an older child to put on her shoes, both of you sign *shoes* as part of the interaction.

Although your baby may not be totally focused on the interaction, the additional exposure in a natural setting is a tremendous influence. The more opportunities Baby has to witness her role models signing, the faster she will adopt Baby Sign Language.

Taking Inventory

Remember to keep track of the words you and your child learn. This means taking a periodic inventory of those signs. Use the worksheets at the end of this book to document each sign learned. Scan your sign inventory weekly to ensure there are no signs that have fallen out of use. If you find unused signs, use them in the coming days to prevent them from being forgotten.

Chapter Six
Signing Phrases

Once Baby builds a basic vocabulary and develops confidence with signing, the next step is combining signs to form phrases. Ideas for combinations include:

- **Familiar Signs** - introduce compound signs by showing Baby how to combine two signs

- **Descriptive & Subject Signs** - help Baby make phrases by adding a description or a subject sign

- **Manners** - encourage courteous behavior by combining *please* and *thank you* with signing requests

Once your baby develops a vocabulary greater than thirty words, challenge him to combine signs. Combining two or more signs is a significant milestone in language development. Combining signs is the first step toward the articulation of phrases and sentences, which is a much more complex form of communication than just using individual words. Many children start combining signs naturally as they develop their sign language skills. The exercises in this chapter will help improve combination signing.

Apes and Sign Language

In the past 50 years, several apes have been taught to sign or use pictograms. Researchers wanted to know if apes are able to use language in the same manner humans do. Some of these apes have developed relatively large vocabularies. For example, Kanzi, a bonobo at the Georgia State University Language Research Center, has a vocabulary of 200 words!

Apes have even demonstrated the ability to improvise, combining old signs in new ways. Washoe, a chimpanzee who was one of the first apes to learn signing, famously improvised the sign *water-bird* to describe a swan he saw in Central Park.

Two significant differences between humans and apes are the inability of apes to combine more than a couple of words and their inability to grasp basic grammar. While human

continued

children naturally grasp the meaning of a
sentence like, "Put the apple in the box," apes
struggle and are as likely to put the apple on
top of the box as they are to put the apple in
the box.

Simple Signing Phrases

The most enjoyable part of signing combinations is the fascinating
insight into the mind of a young child. Your baby will make some
creative and entertaining sign combinations that reveal how she
thinks. As always, encourage creative signing!

Combining Two Familiar Signs

The first step in forming phrases with signs is to combine two
signs your baby already knows. Up to this point, when your child
is eating cheese and wants more, he probably communicated with
one sign or the other. For example, signing only *more* and leaving
you to infer he wants more cheese from the context. Or signing
cheese and leaving you to infer he wants more of the cheese.

As a first step toward communicating using phrases, encourage the
child to combine *more* and *cheese*.

If Baby simply signs *more*, then ask "more cheese?" and make both
signs. We are challenging Baby to make both signs in order to get
what he wants. Some babies understand immediately, while other
babies require a few lessons to grasp the concept.

When challenging Baby to attempt something new, avoid frustrating Baby, but don't give in too easily and allow Baby to give up
without trying.

Sometimes manipulating your baby's fingers will help them understand the concept of combining signs. Observing others model the combination signing can also help Baby make the connection (see Pepperberg Method in *Chapter 5: Advanced Teaching Methods*).

Creative Signs

My youngest signs *good milk* when she wants to nurse instead of drink from a cup. My oldest, at around a year, would sign *pretty bug* for butterfly, and *scared bug* to mean grasshoppers, which he was terrified of!

Sarah E. Bruce

My daughter signs *green tree* for broccoli and signs *fishy cracker* specifically for a goldfish cracker.

Tamara Gibbs

Adding Descriptive Words

Adjectives naturally facilitate combination signing, so learn descriptive words that can be used frequently. Examples of starter adjectives include *big*, *little*, *red*, and *wet*. Popular adjective categories include:

- **Color** - a classic combination is an object and a color. Start with basic colors like *red*, *blue*, *yellow*, *green*, *black*, and *white*, before moving into mixed colors like *purple* and *orange*. Pass the *red ball*. I see a *yellow duck*. You are wearing *blue shoes*.

- **Size** - another good combination is an object and a size. Start with the basic *big* and *little*. For example, a *big dog*.

- **Numbers** - advanced signers that understand numbers and counting can use numbers as adjectives. For example, *two birds*. This is an excellent teaching technique that develops communication and counting skills. Using numbers as descriptors is exciting to children because counting can be used for all sorts of objects in their environment. Baby will love to show off her counting skills by telling you how many birds she sees or how many blocks are in her tower.

- **Sensory** - sensory adjectives that appeal to Baby's developing senses of touch and taste are great to add to known words because the child can experience the sign. For example, *wet diaper*, *noisy car*, *hot cereal*, and *sweet yogurt*.

When teaching descriptive word phrases, utilize contrasting objects so your baby can make a quick comparison. For example, compare a *big ball* and a *little ball*. Or, have a *wet towel* and a *dry towel* handy to let Baby experience the difference.

Adding Subjects

In the early stages of signing, babies learn to sign action words without any accompanying subject. For example, they may sign *eat* or *up* or *bye-bye* without specifying what they want to eat, who they want to pick them up, or to whom they are signing bye-bye. The subject of the action must be inferred from the context.

As your baby progresses, encourage him to use a subject word (noun). Encourage Baby to say *eat cheese*, *up mommy*, and *bye-bye daddy*.

Facilitate the process of adding subjects to actions by signing and saying the complete phrase when Baby only signs a single word. When Baby signs *eat* while pointing at cheese, say and sign "you want to *eat cheese*?" As Baby starts to understand, nudge Baby toward signing the phrase by not fulfilling his request until he signs the phrase.

A Craving Combination

My 19 month old daughter, Madison, had been standing by the front door with my keys in hand for at least 15 minutes frantically signing *food stick* and *eat* over and over again. She never got upset, just more and more determined.

After much guesswork, I finally figured out the *food sticks* she wanted to *eat* are french fries! She had her first fries about a week ago ... I guess she liked them!

I had to reward her for her persistence and ingenuity.

Sarah Bruce

Be Polite

We all know how important it is to instill manners in a young child. You can start early with Baby Sign Language.

Please is a great sign to add to the end of requests. Instead of just signing *cracker* when hungry, Baby can now sign *cracker please*. This teaches Baby to combine signs and introduces good manners. This habit will also expose your baby to the differences between requests and statements.

Remember to be a role model by using please when requesting actions from your baby. Baby learns more from your example than from your instructions.

Ms. Manners

I wanted to be sure my daughter had great manners for the rest of her life. To reinforce the importance, I introduced *please* and *thank you* soon after she started signing at 10 months. Now that she's 3 years old, her manners are in place and signing has become a fun way for us to communicate with each other as well as "show off" and get others interested in the art of signing.

Megan Saxton

Chapter Seven
Signing During the Toddler Years

Baby Sign Language helps reduce the difficulties that often accompany the toddler years. In this chapter we explore a few techniques to reduce toddler frustration. These techniques include:

- **Advance Notice** - inform Baby of upcoming events to avert tantrums

- **Choices** - involve Baby in small decisions to increase Baby's sense of control

- **Listening** - ensure Baby feels heard by better understanding her communication attempts

- **Potty Training** - prepare for potty training by familiarizing Baby with the concept and teaching her to communicate her potty needs

Many parents notice that their toddlers become more temperamental around 18 months of age. This phase of toddler development is popularly referred to as the "terrible twos." Baby Sign Language is immensely helpful during this phase. Signing reduces toddler frustration by increasing the toddler's ability to communicate.

A significant source of a child's frustration is the feeling of helplessness. Without a sense of control, children are prone to "acting out" to release their frustration and anger. This often involves throwing a tantrum in an effort to reassert control over their environment.

Imagine you would like to go to the park and play on the swings. Now imagine you are a baby who cannot talk. You cannot take yourself to the park. Even if you somehow figure out how to tell someone to get you to the park, how would you tell them that it is the swings, not the see-saw that you want to play on. Sounds daunting and frustrating doesn't it? Most of us would give up long before getting to the park. A tantrum might now seem like the logical response.

Lacking control and possessing limited means of communicating with those in control is difficult. Toddlers experience this every day. Combine lack of control with a limited ability to communicate and throw in emotional immaturity and you have the recipe for the "terrible twos."

Communication via signing acts as a liberator for the child. She can interact with her caregivers and receive a response. This productive interaction provides the child with that all-important sense of control. This significantly reduces her frustration and helps makes the twos terrific.

A Note on Empowerment

Parents are often unsure where to draw the line between empowering a child and spoiling a child. By giving a child the ability to communicate early, Baby Sign Language often results in numerous requests. Should all of these requests be fulfilled?

Think of empowerment as giving a child the ability to communicate, make choices, and act freely within boundaries. This reduces frustration and helps transition the child toward adulthood. Empowerment is not giving a child their way every single time.

Boundaries must still be established and respected. Although a child can make requests using Baby Sign Language, you do not need to fulfill all requests. We find that the best way to turn down requests is to acknowledge the request, but respond with a firm "no". "I know you want to play outside, but we can't go outside now." It is important that the request is acknowledged so Baby knows they were understood. It is also important that the "no" is firm and decisive so Baby knows you mean it.

Advance Notice

Informing your child of an upcoming event or action is a powerful way to reduce fussiness. Signing *sleep* or *bedtime* to your child ten minutes before putting her to bed will help her mentally prepare and understand the situation. This is particularly powerful when Baby is able to sign back. Simply knowing what to expect reduces fussiness with most children. Just as most adults prefer to be informed about upcoming events and resent obligations pushed on them at the last minute, children also appreciate a bit of advance notice.

Providing advance notice reduces fussing
by preparing Baby for the transition to follow.

Perhaps your child throws a fit when getting into her car seat. If she understands that you are driving to the park to play with friends on the playground, she might not protest as much. Before getting in the car, prime the child for going to the park and tell her what to expect. "We will get in the *car* and go to the *park*. We are going to play with *friends*, and *swing* at the playground, and we may even see some *birds* or *dogs*." Use a few key signs that your child knows and have the child sign back about what she wants to do at the park.

This technique may also be used to introduce unfamiliar items like a new food. Teach your baby the sign for a new food with a picture or a flash card and establish familiarity. This eases the introduction of the new food and makes Baby more likely to try the food when the opportunity arises. This may not work the first time, but success is more likely after only three or four exposures, instead of nine or ten.

Provide Choices

Choices expand a child's sense of control. Mealtimes are opportunities to provide your child with choices. When feeding your child from your plate, offer her a choice. Let her select *potatoes* or *bread*. Make each sign, showing Baby the options, and ask her to sign the item she chooses.

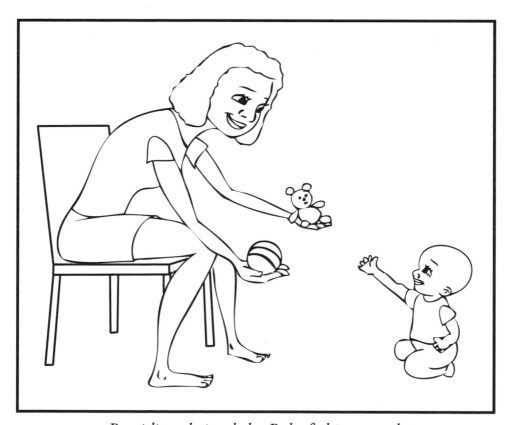

Providing choices helps Baby feel in control.

You can also be a little tricky and give your baby choices that don't particularly matter. For example, if your baby dislikes wearing shoes, minimize the objection by giving her a choice: Do you want to wear the *blue shoes* or the *brown shoes*? This choice allows your baby to participate in the event rather than simply being forced to obey.

Choices should be limited to only a few alternatives. Babies do best with two options. A multitude of choices can be stressful for children and results in confusion.

Do not offer options that you cannot fulfill. While this can be tempting, once you lose their trust it becomes difficult to win back.

Listening

Listening is a skill that most adults have not perfected. Listening requires patience and focus. Frequently, we do not take the time to truly listen to our children. This situation is made worse when a child is unable to effectively communicate. The result is a parent assuming they know what the child is conveying. Baby Sign Language helps facilitate listening because it requires the parent to look directly at the child. When your baby tries to communicate using signs, focus your complete attention on her. This attention will be appreciated and will further confirm the child's realization that sign language is a powerful tool.

Parents are often surprised at how creatively babies can adapt their limited signing vocabulary to communicate successfully. Although this creativity is exciting for a parent to witness, it can be challenging to decode the child's message. To ensure effective communication, repeat the child's sign and speak the word aloud to confirm that the message was received and understood.

Potty Training

Potty training is a case study in the importance of communication. To be potty trained, a child must understand their bodily functions and communicate their needs in a timely manner. Baby Sign Language will help develop that channel of communication. Early preparation with a few signs will establish a strong foundation for potty training success.

The *potty* sign should be learned well before Baby begins potty training. Sign *potty* whenever you use the toilet in front of Baby. Once potty training begins, Baby will already have communication cues associated with using the potty.

Also, learn the signs *diaper*, *wet*, *pee pee*, and *poop* (*poo poo*). Use these signs when changing your baby's diaper. Begin to include such signs as part of your dialogue with Baby. Say and sign "Oh, you have a *wet diaper*. You went *pee pee* in your diaper. Mommy and daddy go *pee pee* in the *potty*. One day soon, you can also go *pee pee* in the *potty*."

This early communication about toilet habits will better prepare your baby for formal potty training. Do not be shy about potty conversations. The goal is to create the tools for communicating about pottying. These conversations help your baby develop a potty-related vocabulary and an awareness of her bodily functions. This minor investment will pay significant dividends once potty training begins.

Chapter Eight
Speaking and Signing

In this chapter we transition from sign language to full vocalization. Topics of focus include:

- **Verbalizing** - the importance of speaking the word while you make the sign

- **Encouraging Speech** - tips for promoting the transition to speech

Baby Sign Language is a springboard for speaking. In fact, when a child encounters difficulty talking, many speech therapists teach the child sign language to facilitate the transition to full speech.

One of the principal frustrations children experience as they begin to talk is that their first words aren't easily understood by adults. When parents do not understand a child attempting to articulate a word or thought, the child becomes frustrated and begins to lose confidence in his speaking ability. However, if the child signs a word as he speaks it, the adult understands what the child is saying. This understanding provides positive reinforcement. Consequently, children that use sign language have greater confidence in their ability to speak.

Additionally, knowing the word the child speaks allows parents to help the child work on proper pronunciation.

Below are some tips on how to use signing to help your baby start talking.

Always Verbalize

Always accompany your signs with the spoken word. The ultimate goal of Baby Sign Language is to help a child communicate by speaking. Pronouncing the word while signing helps your baby learn to articulate the word.

Even if your baby does not repeat the word verbally, the sound is stored away in his memory and will come back to him when he begins to talk. A child understands words and phrases well before he can properly articulate them. Verbalizing at this stage mentally prepares your child to speak before his ability to vocalize is fully developed.

Sign and Word Confusion

In the early months of signing, children often confuse signs of words that sound similar. For example, the sign *doggie* may be confused with *daddy*. This occurs even before children are able to speak. Although you must work to clarify any confusion, this mix-up of similar sounding words shows us that children associate signs with the spoken word.

Babies often confuse signs for similar sounding words.
This confirms they are learning the spoken word as well as the sign.

Encourage Speaking

A Natural Process

Most children naturally start speaking while signing. There is typically a lengthy overlap period when your child is both signing and speaking. Signs during this phase are often easier to understand than the spoken word. Therefore, signing serves as the dominant mode of communication while your baby's voice develops. Encourage signing during this phase of language development to improve communication.

As your child's speaking skills improve, he will naturally transition toward speech. Speaking is easier and faster than signing for your child. Speaking is also the primary mode of communication for most families.

This transition process usually happens automatically. Since you are simultaneously speaking and signing, your baby is learning to verbalize at the same time they are learning to sign.

Promote Speaking

Speech development begins much like signing development. Start by choosing a few words that are relevant to the child, easy to pronounce, and frequently used. Select words that your baby is verbalizing, but not yet mastered. When your child uses a sign without attempting to speak the word, speak the word to him. "Cheese, you want cheese?" "Say cheese." Then only let the child have the cheese if he attempts to say the word.

Some children initially dislike using words because speaking is difficult. They prefer to take shortcuts such as grabbing or pointing. The job of parents, teachers, and caregivers is to challenge the child to speak. Perfect pronunciation is not the objective. The objective is simply to encourage the child to attempt the word.

*Encourage the transition by asking Baby
to say the word along with the sign.*

Do not give in to temper tantrums. It is counterproductive for a child to believe a tantrum helps him achieve his objective. Conversely, avoid a battle of wills. If your child is frustrated or fussy, he is not in a good state for learning. When your child is unable to speak a word and grows increasingly frustrated, turn his attention to something else.

During the transitional phase, encourage your child to sign while he attempts to speak. Deciphering those initial spoken words is easier when you have the accompanying signs. Signs allow you to recognize early attempts at speaking and therefore provide encouragement. Additionally, your child's frustration is reduced as he is understood even when just learning to talk.

As children get older and more articulate, focus on proper pronunciation and usage. Initially, parents are excited that Baby says "ah" for "ball," but progression requires parents to gradually raise the bar and encourage proper articulation. First, emphasize the leading sound. Say "buh, buh, ball." Once your child masters the "b" sound, emphasize the ending "l" sound. Say "ball luh luh ball."

Avoid "baby talk." Incorrect pronunciation is a natural phase of language development, but it should not be rewarded or promoted by the parent. If your child says "lellow" instead of "yellow," emphasize the "y" sound and practice with your child in a positive and encouraging manner. Recall how you handled signing approximations, acknowledging Baby's rudimentary sign with encouragement while reinforcing correct usage. Apply the same principle to verbal communication to avoid reinforcing speech pathologies. "Baby talk" is cute, but we want to progress to proper pronunciation.

Chapter Nine
Signing
Beyond Babyhood

Once your child becomes fully verbal, there are many opportunities to continue signing. These opportunities include:

- **Teaching** - older children use their sign language skills to teach younger siblings

- **Secret Code** - sign language can be used for private or silent communication between you and your child

- **Continuing Education** - achieve signing proficiency by taking classes, signing along to songs or videos, or practicing with proficient signers

There are many opportunities to use sign language even after your child enters preschool and transitions to talking. Like most skills, sign language will be forgotten if not used. Fortunately, sporadic use of sign language will ensure your child retains the skill.

Teaching Siblings

Older children often teach younger siblings how to sign. Teaching a younger child is a wonderful activity for older children, particularly if they are only a few years old themselves. Teaching creates a sense of authority and allows the older sibling to feel grown-up. Allowing older siblings to teach their little brother or sister also strengthens their relationship and reduces their need to compete for parental attention.

Kids learn faster from their peers than their parents. Of course, this can be a source for parental stress when they are older, but you can reap the benefits of peer-to-peer learning now.

Help your little assistant coach along by giving her a few tips. Ensure she focuses on a few basic signs at first, forms the signs slowly, and repeats the signs often. But even without any instruction, you will be surprised at how well they do!

Secret Code

Both kids and adults are suckers for a good secret. Sign language allows parents and kids to create their own private code of communication. Signing an inside joke while out in public is a lot of fun. And because only you and your child are privy to the conversation, it is especially enjoyable. Signing is also a useful way to communicate when speaking would be disruptive. For example, if your child needs to use the restroom during a church service or movie, she can communicate the need without disrupting others.

Some children prefer to use sign language when they are outside of their comfort zone. For example, if your child is sick and visiting the pediatrician, she may feel more comfortable signing than speaking. Children often become shy when they encounter new adults, so encourage them to use signs while they develop the confidence to speak.

If your child occasionally forgets her manners and needs a little reminder, signing lets you provide a gentle nudge without embarrassing her. If your child forgets to say "thank you" at grandma's house, flashing a quick *thank you* sign will remind her to say the magic words that make grandma happy. Or if your child is playing rough at the playground, you can flash a quick *stop* sign.

Sign language lets you discretely communicate delicate matters.
(Mommy is asking Baby if she needs to "potty",
we will let you figure out the response)

A note of caution: Avoid signing only in negative situations (i.e., when correcting your child's behavior). An occasional reminder is fine, followed by a quick smile or *thank you* once she follows your instruction. Also, incorporate signs into fun activities to ensure your child associates signing with positive experiences.

Continuing Education

ASL Class

American Sign Language (ASL) classes are a fantastic opportunity to expand signing vocabularies and refine signing skills. Classes are typically offered through your local association for the deaf or community college. ASL classes are also a great way to meet like-minded signers.

ASL Grammar

If you want to learn official American Sign Language (ASL), you will discover that ASL grammar and sentence structure differs from spoken English. For example, ASL sentences usually start with the time, then the topic of the sentence, and then a comment on that topic. Instead of saying that "I went to the mall yesterday", you would sign "Yesterday-mall-I-went."

To learn more about ASL Grammar check out www.lifeprint.com/asl101/pages-layout/grammar.htm

Songs and Videos

Kids love to sign along to their favorite song. Signing along to a DVD is more interactive and engaging than simply watching. Television shows that incorporate ASL with singing are a great signing activity. You can also turn any of your child's favorite songs or movies into a signing opportunity by selecting a few words to sign once they appear on the screen.

For older children, there are a number of contemporary songs with the accompanying ASL on YouTube. Just search for "ASL" plus the song or artist of your choice.

Practice With the Pros

Practicing with proficient signers is the ideal method to advance sign language skills. If your children have friends who use sign language, encourage them to sign during play dates. Signing quickly becomes smoother and faster when your child interacts with experienced signers.

Conclusion

We hope this book gets you started on your Baby Sign Language journey and is one of the first steps on the grander journey of nurturing your child to adulthood. One of the privileges of teaching Baby Sign Language is seeing the different paths that a child can take. Children respond to different teaching methods, learn at different rates, and gravitate to different parts of the Baby Sign Language program. As you embark on this journey, we encourage you to focus on the experience of connecting with your child.

Strive to identify what spurs your child to learn, what material engages him, and which techniques are most effective. Does he prefer direct teaching or modeling? Is he more interested in animals or food? What time of day is optimal for learning, and how long are effective teaching sessions? What is frustrating, and what is exciting? The answers to these questions are valuable for teaching more than just Baby Sign Language.

Also reflect on how you teach. Do you gravitate toward specific teaching methods and avoid others? Do your preferred teaching methods align with your child's learning style? What inspires you to teach, and what frustrates you?

In the first few years of your child's life you are laying the foundation for your future relationship. When your child grows up and goes out into the world, the time you spent together learning Baby Sign Language will probably be a distant memory. However, the mentor relationship you create is an investment in his future and will shape the path for development long after the infant and toddler years have passed.

The goal of this book is to create a structured approach to a transformational development opportunity. This development extends well beyond communication and into the relationship between a child and parent. Enjoy the experience of teaching your child Baby Sign Language. We are privileged to be part of your signing experience and welcome questions, success stories, and additional tips for teaching Baby Sign Language.

E-mail us at book@babysignlanguage.com, connect with us through our website at www.BabySignLanguage.com, or join our Facebook community at www.facebook.com/babysignlang.

Worksheets

Use the worksheets on the following pages to keep track of new signs. Record the date you first introduced the new sign, the date Baby first repeated the sign, and the date Baby mastered the new sign (i.e., correctly initiated the sign in context).

These worksheets help you track progress and remind you how much your baby has achieved. The worksheets also show the composition of Baby's vocabulary. Review the worksheets to identify gaps, then introduce words that augment Baby's vocabulary.

Periodically review the worksheets to ensure that all signs are occasionally used. If a sign has not been used recently, use it with Baby to ensure the sign is not forgotten.

Sign	Introduced	Imitated	Mastered

Sign	Introduced	Imitated	Mastered

Sign	Introduced	Imitated	Mastered

Sign	Introduced	Imitated	Mastered

Sign	Introduced	Imitated	Mastered